MW00354526

O. Henry

O. HENRY

(William Sidney Porter)

CHARLES ALPHONSO SMITH, Ph. D., LL. D.

BIOGRAPHER

PREPARED FOR THE

LIBRARY *of* SOUTHERN LITERATURE

THE MARTIN AND HOYT COMPANY

Atlanta, Georgia

O. HENRY

(William Sidney Porter)

CHARLES ALPHONSO SMITH, Ph.D., LL.D., L. H. D.
BIOGRAPHER

In the Series of Southern Authors

No. 277 Compiled Under the Direct Supervision of Southern Men of Letters for the

LIBRARY OF SOUTHERN LITERATURE

Editor in Chief
EDWIN ANDERSON ALDERMAN, LL.D.
President University of Virginia

THE MARTIN AND HOYT COMPANY
Atlanta, Georgia

O. HENRY
(William Sidney Porter)

"In the Bible of births kept by O. Henry's father, it is recorded that on September 11, 1862, there was born at 9 o'clock P. M., William Sidney Porter. But in the latter part of his life O. Henry spelled it Sydney."

O. HENRY

[1862—1910]

C. ALPHONSO SMITH

I

IF the work of William Sidney Porter, better known as O. Henry, was the most noteworthy contribution made to American literature during the first decade of the twentieth century, the expanding vogue of that work has no less characterized the succeeding decade. He was hardly a national author at the time of his death in 1910, but in 1920 he seems securely national and international. The largest class of midshipmen at the United States Naval Academy was recently asked to name in writing the author whose complete works, if placed in the library of every American battleship, would be most often called for. O. Henry led by two hundred votes, Mark Twain coming second. It will be recalled also that at the autograph sales held in New York at the American Art Galleries early in 1918 a twelve-page letter from O. Henry, already published, sold for $810, while an unpublished autobiographical manuscript by Mark Twain, consisting of fourteen pages, brought only $540. "If I had discovered him before his death," wrote Sir James M. Barrie, "I should have considered a trip to the United States well worth while to make his acquaintance." But nothing ever said of O. Henry would have pleased him more than a sentence from a London paper during the great war: "We ought to be reading our casualty lists, for God knows they are heavy enough; but, instead, we are all reading O. Henry." The appreciation of O. Henry came to England, however, only after effort. "It was not easy for the British public to 'get' O. Henry at first," said Sir Ernest Hodder Williams during his recent visit to New York. "They had to try. But they've got him now, and all over England you hear O. Henry being quoted."

The World War, by the way, was a severe test to the popularity of writers, living and dead, American and European. It brought in a new audience, with new interests, with changed or changing ideals, with a refashioned outlook. Ordinary appeals seemed exhausted, for the world had been reduced to the bare elementals again. But the elemental facts of human nature, the essential traits of the human heart, are precisely those that gave O. Henry both theme and arena. O. Henry entered Europe *via* the French trenches because the French trenches spelled the common denominator of human nature. "O. Henry was our greatest literary discovery during the war," writes John o'London.[1] "He was medicinal. He distracted us from intolerable things. His name is as familiar as that of Kipling, Conan Doyle, or Jacobs." Writing of actual life in the trenches Frank A. Lewis[2] reports that, when *Options* was received, "an hour of insane jubilation ensued." The book was torn at once into its seventeen separate stories, the pages were pinned together, and seventeen soldiers feasted synchronously on seventeen stories instead of successively on one volume. Of course the war served to postpone the translation of O. Henry into foreign tongues; but he can now be read in German, Swedish, Dano-Norwegian, French, Spanish, and Japanese. When we add to this that five million volumes of his stories have been sold and that his vogue is steadily increasing among readers of all classes, it need hardly be reaffirmed that the chief current in American literature from 1910 to 1920 has been that issuing from the stories written by O. Henry in the ten years preceding.

II

O. Henry's life falls into four clearly marked stages, each stage contributing a definite quota to his training and a distinctive flavor to his writing.

(1) He was born in Greensboro, North Carolina, September 11, 1862 (not 1867), where he remained until 1882, and where the O. Henry Hotel now testifies to the local esteem in which his memory is held. His schooling was limited, but his reading was wide and avid. "I did more reading," he said, "between my thirteenth and nineteenth years than I have ever done in all the years since, and my taste at that time was much better than it is now, for I used to read nothing but the classics. Burton's *Anatomy of Melancholy* and Lane's translation of *The Arabian Nights* were my favorites." A count of all the books and authors referred to by him in his stories shows that the great Perso-Arabian classic stands well among the first. The Bible leads with sixty-three references. Shakespeare follows with thirty-four; Tennyson with twenty-one; *The Arabian Nights* with fourteen; Kipling with twelve; Byron and Dickens with seven each; Omar Khayyam with six; Conan Doyle with five; Cæsar, Marcus Aurelius, Keats, and Henry James each with four. The total number of authors alluded to directly or indirectly is one hundred and twenty-three, the number of references being three hundred and thirty-six. But O. Henry took with him from Greensboro not only a love of good books but an ability as a humorous cartoonist that gave evidence, before the age of ten, of rare constructive and interpretative talent. The man who was later to be acclaimed as the short story historian of New York City began by being the annalist of Greensboro through his cartoons.

(2) From 1882 to 1896 he lived in Texas, first on a ranch, then in

---

[1] See *The New York Times Book Review*, May 16, 1920.
[2] *The Publishers' Weekly*, Philadelphia, December 8, 1917.

Austin, then in Houston, with occasional visits to San Antonio. His out-of-doors life on the plains gave material that was afterwards to appear not only in pictorial description and vivid narrative but in a wealth of first-hand observation, in a widening of personal experience, and in a breaking away from mere bookishness, that find illustration in every page of his *Heart of the West*. It was not a summer visitor that wrote that book. It was one who had lived the life and loved it; it was one who needed just this wider horizon to give him margin for comparison with what had gone before and basis for contrast with what was to come later. His reading partook now more of the nature of study. He mastered Spanish, pored over the great historians that he found in a ranch library, pitted his narrative art against theirs, and learned in constant comradeship with Webster's Unabridged Dictionary an accuracy and freedom in the use of words that random reading could not give. During these seven years also he practised the cartoonist's art as before, not, so far as I can learn, with a view to utilizing it, but merely for the pleasure that he found in some form of disciplined self-expression. In Austin he edited *The Rolling Stone* and in Houston he contributed *Postscripts and Pencillings* to the *Daily Post*.

(3) The third stage, that from July, 1896, to July, 1901, made him what he became, not only a master of the short story, but a thinker about human life, a delver into its mysteries, an appraiser of its conflicts, a noble exemplar of its hidden but unconquerable reserves. Out of these five years was wrought the philosophy that makes *The World and the Door* a permanent contribution to the literature of humanitarian reform. For more than six months of this time he was a wanderer, "a fugitive from justice"—so the indictment runs—in Central and South America. The charge was that, while acting as paying and receiving teller in the First National Bank of Austin, he had misappropriated funds, a charge not only baseless but susceptible of easy disproof had not a whim of the moment sped him on his fateful and compromising tour among the Latin-Americans. Returning to Austin to nurse his dying wife, O. Henry surrendered himself to the authorities, asserted his innocence of the charge made against him, and after a brief trial was sentenced to the federal prison in Columbus, Ohio. He entered the prison on April 25, 1898, and without a demerit against him was released on July 24, 1901. It was here that he wrote his first twelve stories and assumed the now famous pseudonym, O. Henry. The name was taken without change from the *United States Dispensatory* which he used when he was a drug clerk in Greensboro, Austin, and Columbus. It is the abbreviation of the name of a famous French pharmacist, Etienne-Ossian Henry.[1]

(4) From Columbus O. Henry went at once to Pittsburgh, Pennsylvania, where his daughter and her grandparents were then living. But

[1] See *The Nation*, New York, May 11, 1918; *The State Journal*, Raleigh, North Carolina, May 31, 1918; *Nouvelles de France*, Paris, July 25, 1918; *The Daily News*, Greensboro, North Carolina, "O. Henry Edition," July 2, 1919.

in the spring of 1902 he moved to New York City, where he died on June 5, 1910. He was buried in Asheville, North Carolina, the home of his second wife, where he had sought and seemingly found restoration to health and where his grave is visited annually by many thousands of devoted tourists. It was in New York that O. Henry's genius culminated, though he did not devote himself wholeheartedly to the absorption and reproduction of the great city until he had harvested his Latin-American experiences by the publication in November, 1904, of *Cabbages and Kings*. His real flowering period began in December, 1903, when he signed a contract with *The New York World* for a story a week. The price was a hundred dollars a story. The responsibility thus imposed, with all that it promised of release from need and uncertainty, was a challenge that evoked for the first time in his life every ounce of energy and determination that he possessed. His training had been varied and thorough, and the passion for self-expression that had burned in him from childhood found now a happy and adequate outlet. "The city teaches the man," said Simonides. It not only taught O. Henry, but released in him the powers and appetencies that had before been cramped or caged. During the first month of his contract he contributed not only the required four stories to *The Sunday World*, but one each to *Ainslee's*, *McClure's*, and *Everybody's*. This amazing quota of seven stories he repeated in February, May, and December of the following year. A marked falling off in the number but not in the quality of his stories becomes noticeable early in 1907. Ill health had gripped him and inspiration lagged. His total output of stories, if we omit fragments and early extravaganzas, is two hundred and fifty.

III

"Grammar, to O. Henry," says an English critic,[1] "was only one way of saying a thing. He had others equally efficient when he wanted, for he was a master, and not a servant, of words. For two years in Texas his favourite companion was a dictionary—which he studied as lovingly as some men study poetry." O. Henry was a conformist and a non-conformist; but conformity and non-conformity were governed by the same law, the law of effect. Few writers knew words better than he or felt more instinctively their limitations as well as their possibilities. Words had more than meaning to O. Henry: they had flavor, a flavor unknown to Noah Webster, but recognized by every poet and prose writer who has enriched the resources of our speech. To most writers the dictionary says "You must," to O. Henry it said "You may," and the freedom thus imparted has contributed no little of the sparkle and humor and suggestiveness of O. Henry's vocabulary.

He had no pet words, at least no pet coinages, if we except "accusive." The word is not found in any dictionary, but it is so aptly used by

---

[1] See *The Spectator*, London, April 7, 1917.

O. Henry—in "accusive eyes," "accusive talk", "accusive silence"—that it deserves a place in the dictionaries of the future. His mastery is seen, however, not only in new formations but in new uses. He writes of "the petitionary music of a violin," the rattle of cabs and "the snarling of the electric cars," "the stale infestivity of a table d'hôte," "a flashy fellow with a predatory eye," a tramp obeying his surly master "with propitiatory alacrity," "the priceless and induplicable flag," a woman tiding over "the vast chasms of nicotinized silence" with music from her guitar, an atmosphere "international with cigarette smoke," "cheap fellows, sonorously garbed," a man "with salamandrous thumbs, serving the scalding viands." These words are all in the lexicographer's stable but the harnessing is O. Henry's.

When O. Henry takes liberties with the form of words rather than with their meanings, his so-called audacities suggest comparison with those that Sheridan immortalized in the speech of Mrs. Malaprop. But there is a fundamental difference. Mrs. Malaprop says: You must "illiterate him quite from your memory"; don't try "to extirpate yourself"; he is "a progeny of learning"; a certain woman does not "reprehend the true meaning of what she is saying"; I laid "my positive conjunctions on her never to think on the fellow again"; someone is as headstrong as "an allegory on the banks of the Nile," etc. These are blunders adroitly chosen by Sheridan, but they are nothing more than blunders. They cause laughter, but they do not quicken thought. They belong in the same class with the verbal mutilations of Mrs. Slipslop in Fielding's *Joseph Andrews*.

But O. Henry's audacities mark a distinct advance. Instead of making nonsense they suggest sense. Apart from their humor they often drive home the intended idea with a vividness impossible to any other words. Compare the malapropisms already cited with these O. Henryisms: There was an Indian Territory feud of which I was press-agent, camp-follower, and "inaccessory during the fact"; it was a large, conglomerate building, "presided under by a janitor"; the third day of the rain, Andy walked out to the edge of the town "to view the mudscape"; he was a fierce little old man who "regarded himself as especial mastiff-in-waiting to protect the two young artists"; the duty of the Statue of Liberty Enlightening the World is "to offer a cast-ironical welcome to the oppressed of other lands"; for table-talk and fireside companions, sheep "rank along with five-o'clock teazers"; if you know anything about the thief, "you are amiable to the law in not reporting it"; it [a town named Guayaquerita] is a clear case where Spelling Reform "ought to butt in and disenvowel it"; Clara, the negro servant, spoke in tones "half-contemptuous, half-Tuskegeenial."

O. Henry's made or misused words, like Sheridan's and Fielding's, resemble in sound the canonical words, but instead of having no meaning they are made to carry a new meaning. We laugh not merely because standardized forms have been unceremoniously shattered, but because out of the fragments there suddenly emerges a new and unexpected idea. In Sheridan we admire the brilliant consistency with which Mrs. Malaprop's arrows fall wide of the mark. In O. Henry we admire the added cleverness that speeds the arrow not to its conventional target, it is true, but not to the ground; it glances from its goal and strikes squarely another target which we did not know was in that neighborhood. Mrs. Malaprop mutilates; O. Henry transmutes.

A similar difference is seen between O. Henry's cleverest misquotations and the misquotations of other humorists. A study of the question would show, I think, three general stages in the art of humorous misquotation. The first stage is illustrated by Chaucer's rooster who flatters and pacifies his wife at the end of a long controversy by telling her:

> For, also siker as *In principio*,
> *Mulier est hominis confusio.*
> Madame, the sentence of this Latin is—
> Womman is mannes joye and al his blis.

Here there is no tampering with the quoted words. They are given accurately by Chauntecleer, liberty being taken with the translation rather than with the quotation proper. O. Henry rarely attempts this kind of inversion, though his most notable example happens to be drawn, as was Chaucer's, from a Latin quotation. Thus Henry Horsecollar is made to say: "Then we'll export canned music to the Latins; but I'm mindful of Mr. Julius Cæsar's account of 'em where he says: 'Omnis Gallia in tres partes divisa est'; which is the same as to say, 'We will need all of our gall in devising means to tree them parties.'" The second stage in the evolution of effective misquotation brings Mrs. Malaprop again to the fore. She differs from Chauntecleer in quoting inaccurately but, as before, no new meaning or application is superadded to the quotation as a whole. As in the case of individual words, Sheridan makes her blunder and blunder egregiously, but there is no scintillation from the blunder. It is mere mutilation. "Then his presence," she says, "is so noble! I protest when I saw him, I thought of what Hamlet says in the play:—'Hesperian curls—the front of Job himself!—an eye, like March, to threaten at command!—a station, like Harry Mercury, new—'? Something about kissing—on a hill—however, the similitude struck me directly."

In the third stage, O. Henry's priority and primacy seem to me equally assured. Jeff Peters, for example, in explanation of how he and another gentle grafter lost their booty, remarks: "We were self-curbed. It was a case of auto-suppression. There was a rift within the loot, as Albert Tennyson says." In another passage Jeff tells how a mine owner, having lost his fortune, climbs to the top of a house and jumps off on a spot "where he now requiescats in pieces." Andy Tucker, Jeff's partner, wants to go to the Riviera for leisure and meditation: "I want to loaf and indict my soul, as Walt Whittier says." A connoisseur in the ordering of fashionable dinners is described as one "to the menu born." Spenser's famous warning in *The Faerie Queene*, "Be bolde, be bolde, and everywhere be bolde. Be not too bolde," is changed into "Be bold; everywhere be bold, but be not bowled over." "A straw vote," says O. Henry, "only shows which way the hot air blows." "Strong drink," we are assured, "is an adder and subtractor, too." A perfect example of the difference between autocracy and democracy is seen in O. Henry's metamorphosis of Tennyson's line into "the fierce light that beats upon the thrown-down." Many other examples might be given, but enough have been cited to show that in forays of this sort O. Henry's endeavor was to bring home a new message from time worn expressions. He pours new wine into old bottles. This is essentially different from Chaucer's practice and from Sheridan's. O. Henry tries to be re-constructive where they are usually content to be negative or destructive.

But O. Henry's humor is not at bottom verbal. It does not inhere in tricks of style or in mannerisms of phrase. He had only one mannerism, a way of massing alliteration. With the poets alliteration is chiefly a matter of euphony; but O. Henry uses it to condense, to heighten, to intensify, to lift quantity or quality into quick and vivid saliency. It takes the place of more elaborate description as well as of more detailed enumeration. When he says the outing was to include "parks, picnics, and Pilsener," I detect an almost parsimonious economy of words. When he describes the cattlemen of an older day as "grandees of the grass, kings of the kine, lords of the lea, barons of beef and bone," I feel that nouns cunningly marshaled have beat adjectives even at the adjectival game. When he declares that "the Madness of Manhattan, the Frenzy of Fuss and Feathers, the Bacillus of Brag, the Provincial Plague of Pose seized upon Towers Chandler," I know that Towers is in for a fall. When he pits an empty-headed Apollo against a suave tongue and adds: "It's the larynx that the beauty doctors ought to work on. It's words more than warts, talk more than talcum, palaver more than powder, blarney more than bloom that counts—the phonograph instead of the photograph," I am convinced as by a deluge of cogent argumentation. When Mrs. Widdup is introduced as "fair, flustered, forty, and foxy," I know her and know her unforgettably both exteriorly and interiorly.

But O. Henry's humor is only marginally a thing of words and phrases. Coruscation, in other words, was with O. Henry merely the · by-product of creation. It was never central or controlling. His characters are not humorous because they say funny things. They say funny things because they are humorous. O. Henry's humor has been acclaimed by a world of grateful readers because, like the humor of Shakespeare and Molière and Cervantes, it rises naturally and spontaneously from the situations in which his characters are placed. The situations become themselves creative; they belong to the elemental nature of comedy. They are matrix rather than mould, and the humor is born rather than made. Review the situations in *The Handbook of Hymen, A Cosmopolite in a Café, The Brief Début of Tildy, A Lickpenny Lover, Two Renegades, The Gift of the Magi, The Cop and the Anthem, Makes the Whole World Kin, The Lady Higher Up, The Pendulum, The Making of a New Yorker.* In each of these the stage is set by a master. There is subtle thought, even profound thought, not so much in the working out of the plots as in the selection and forestaging of such humorous situations as make the plots work themselves out. Humor is released rather than manufactured. It plays hide and seek with pathos in many of these stories and not infrequently both humor and pathos come before the footlights hand in hand to receive the plaudits of an audience that finds it hard to say which is which.

A special distinction of O. Henry's humor is that it is never divisive. On the contrary, it fuses and re-unites. As soon as you read one of his stories you want to read it aloud to others. But you do not have to pick your audience for fear that feelings will be hurt. Rich or poor, educated or illiterate, employer or employee, black or white, man or woman—all will find their common heritage of humanity reached and enriched. Much of the stage humor of today, certainly that of the school of Wilde and Shaw, derives most of its sparkle from what has been called "the neat reversal of middle-class conceptions." There is no such reversal in O. Henry. Instead of pitting class against class he reveals class to class. In *Mammon and the Archer,* for example, it would be hard to say which is the more human and lovable, Aunt Ellen, who is gentle and sentimental and spiritual, or Anthony Rockwall, the retired manufacturer and proprietor of Rockwall's Eureka Soap, who "bets his money on money every time." Read the story and try to make the award. In *The Handbook of Hymen,* the matter-of-fact man is contrasted with the ultra-imaginative man, the statistical with the poetical mind. In its two leading characters the story is a sort of miniature *Don Quixote:* Sanderson Pratt, like Sancho Panza, is the factualist; Idaho Green, like the Knight de la Mancha, is the romanticist. But the balances swing impartial at the end. Neither devotee is derided. The theme is illuminated, but the two contestants are awarded equal honors by the reader. Both characters are extremists, but they are too human, too much like you and me, for O. Henry's ridicule to fall on either.

In *The Duplicity of Hargraves, Best Seller, The Rose of Dixie,* and *Thimble, Thimble,* O. Henry sets himself the task of staging the traditional differences between the Southerner and the Northerner. The subject was a delicate one, but there is no tincture of prejudice in the portrayal. Is not O. Henry the only one of our fictionists in whose hands regional differences never curdle into sectional differences? He finds his differential and makes it clear as day, but Yankee and Southerner join equally in the laughter. The differential is seen to be but a rill in the river of our common humanity; it discloses but it neither dissevers nor discredits. *Makes the Whole World Kin* is the title of only one of O. Henry's stories, but it sums the service of them all.

One element in O. Henry's art seems not to have been touched on by the critics, an element that is as distinctive as his humor. I mean the way in which he saturates his stories with the atmosphere of the background. The French call it *milieu*, the Germans *stimmung*, but O. Henry has added something to both. I do not refer now to the larger geographical backgrounds. It goes without saying that his Latin-American stories are accurately Latin-American, that his New York stories have the New York atmosphere, that his Western stories are distinctively Western, and that his Southern stories have the flavor of the South. But O. Henry goes further than this. He circumscribes his *locale* and makes it a perceptible force in the development of the story. Rooms, boarding houses, hotels, stores, cafés, restaurants, ranches, parks, squares, streets, and street intersections are almost human in O. Henry. If they do not speak, they have life, character, temperament. Stories are commonly divided into three parts, background or setting, character or characters, plot or plan; and the first is thought of as the stationary *locale* where the story takes place. In many stories the *locale* is mentioned at the beginning and then dismissed. Not so in O. Henry's pages. His backgrounds are no more initial than terminal. They are continuous. They constitute a felt presence in the conduct of the characters. O. Henry was not only a student of environment; he was an interpreter of character in its relations to environment. He read men and women in their context. This is why it is so difficult to re-tell an O. Henry story effectively. We name the characters, we summarize the plot, we explain the point of it all, we say where the story takes place. But something has gone out of it. That something is the encompassing and vitalizing background. When we have mentioned or described the *locale*, we are done with it. But in the story it was inwrought into the very texture of the style. It conditioned the talk; it flavored the adjectives; it nominated the nouns; it moved with the verbs. Try to re-tell *The Brief Début of Tildy,* a perfectly simple plot, but so shot through with the restaurant atmosphere that to omit it is to omit the integration of the plot itself.

O. Henry touches upon this theme in *A Matter of Mean Elevation:* "It has been named 'environment,' which is as weak a word as any to express the unnamable kinship of man to nature, that queer fraternity that causes stones and trees and salt water and clouds to play upon our emotions. Why are we made serious and solemn and sublime by mountain heights, grave and contemplative by an abundance of overhanging trees, reduced to inconstancy and monkey capers by the ripples on a sandy beach?" But the environment into which O. Henry pushes his prow are man-made rather than nature-made. Run through a dozen or more of his stories with this thought of environment as one of the co-operant characters in the unfolding of the incidents. If you do not crown O. Henry as the laureate of the background, you will at least be put in the way of having your own powers of correlate observation enriched as by a sixth sense. If you have time for but one story in this quest, go at once to *The Furnished Room* (in *The Four Million*). To my mind it is O. Henry's greatest story, though there is no humor in it. But it is environments probed to its ultimate depth; it is Poe in all his "totality of effect"; it is Hawthorne when he wrote *The House of the Seven Gables;* it is Shakespeare when he set the weird sisters upon the heath to croak the curtained doom of Macbeth.

But notice that in O. Henry environment never, as so often in Thomas Hardy, compels character. It co-operates with it, it releases it, it trains it, at times it checks it. But man is still the master of his fate. Environment may help or hinder; it may not subjugate. O. Henry's own life is a radiant example of how adversity may be reversed, how a stumbling block may be transmuted into a stepping stone. Like the good witch, O. Henry read the spell of an unjust prison sentence backwards and made a fairy appear instead of a goblin. If in *Roads of Destiny,* written in 1903, he seems to lean to the theory of the immalleable environment, remember that three years later he grapples again with the theme in *The Roads We Take* and has Bob Tidball sum it all up in the words: "It ain't the roads we take; it's what's inside of us that makes us turn out the way we do."

In the matter of technique proper, much has been written of the art with which O. Henry holds in suspense the full meaning of his stories till the very end. "On the technical side of his craft," writes the English critic already quoted,[1] "he has probably never been surpassed either in fertility or ingenuity." But the critics have overlooked the art of O. Henry's beginnings. It is the masterly beginning that makes possible the masterly ending, and the ending cannot be properly appraised unless viewed in relation to the beginning. "The flower was unexpected," says Goethe, "even surprising, if you will; but it had to come. The green leaves existed only for it, and without it the leaves would not have been there." Craftsmanship with O. Henry was largely a relation between first words and last words. It had to do, far more than has been thought, with the proper placing of expository matter. Should it come first or last? This was the subject of one of O. Henry's latest conversations about his craft. In one of his stories, after a page and a half of initial explanation, he says, "All this recitative by the chorus is only to bring us to the point where you may be told why," etc. The real purpose of the "recitative by the chorus" is to release a clean, unincumbered ending. When the job is done, he wants neither shavings nor dust left over. "A story with a moral appended," he remarks at the beginning of *The Gold That Glittered*, "is like the bill of a mosquito. It bores you, and then injects a stinging drop to irritate your conscience. Therefore let us have the moral first and be done with it." But why have it at all? Because the end requires

---

[1] *The Spectator*, London, April 7, 1917.

it. In *The Gift of the Magi,* the moral comes last. The real surprise
in this wonderful story is not in what the lovers do at the last; it is in
what O. Henry says about what they do. He congratulates them. They
acted wisely. Their gifts were prompted by love, and the love shines all
the more resplendent because the gifts as gifts could not be used. They
could be treasured as memorials of a devotion that was selfless in its
purpose and unsparing in its effort. But all this belongs to the moral
rather than to the plot, and it could not have come first without de-
priving the plot of its terminal unexpectedness. The projected surprise
was latent in the title. The theme is not the *gifts* of the magi: it is
love, the *gift* of the magi, and the last paragraph tells us so.

O. Henry's usual practice, however, is to place the moral, the nature
of the theme, the expository matter, first, so that the story may end
without the *anhang* of concluding remarks. Note the ending in *A
Municipal Report,* "I wonder what's doing in Buffalo!" This would be
meaningless unless O. Henry had with pre-visioning care given the
clue at the beginning. The story is meant to show that not only New
York and New Orleans and San Francisco but all other cities have
narrative and dramatic possibilities. Where there is actual life there
is potential literature. Turn again to *An Unfinished Story,* one of those
that made Colonel Roosevelt say: "All the reforms that I attempted
in behalf of the working girls of New York were suggested by the
writings of O. Henry." The dynamic ending is made possible only by
the most careful charging of the battery at the beginning. In fact the
story proper is thrust between the beginning and the ending of a dream,
and the reverberation at the close is merely the quick coming together
of the two parts after the lightning has flashed between. In *Roads of
Destiny* there is a different ending for each of the three roads tra-
versed, but each ending couches in the great question with which the
story begins:

> I go to seek on many roads
>   What is to be.
> True heart and strong, with love to light—
> Will they not bear me in the fight
> To order, shun or wield or mould
>   My Destiny?

In the stories, therefore, that discuss or illumine a definite theme,
as most of O. Henry's stories do, the carefully concealed surprise at
the end is to be credited more to skill in ordered exposition than to
any trick of narration or artificiality of structure. The strategy em-
ployed belongs more to the expositor in O. Henry than to the narrator.
He had not so much a tale to tell as a truth to expound, a new point
of view to impress, a novel suggestion to make, a complexity of human
nature to unravel, an obscure motive to illumine, a daring reach of
imaginative sympathy to achieve, and the story partakes of the nature
of a modern parable. Surprise, therefore, is hardly the right word to ex-

press the reader's sensation when he finishes a story of this sort. Recognition would be a better word, recognition of the bearing of part upon part, of totality in place of mere successiveness, of convergence instead of parallelism, of the end as the child of the beginning. Surprise is usually an accompaniment of this kind of recognition, but the pleasure is more in the recognition of the author's masterly adaptation than in the surprise itself.

IV

No sketch of O. Henry is complete without a reference to the man that was in the artist. It was my privilege to know him intimately till at the age of twenty he left North Carolina for Texas. We fished together, seined, hunted, camped out, and serenaded together, and the memory of his personality is as rich a heritage as the treasury of his genius. A few letters from him in Texas, some intermittent copies of *The Rolling Stone*, a long interview in New York when he was at the height of his fame—these are almost my only first-hand memorials after he had exchanged our common birthplace, Greensboro, for the Texas ranch. But there was no essential change. O. Henry was still Will Porter. As I waited for him in the lobby of a New York hotel in 1908, I doubted whether I should even know him. Twenty-six years had passed and to him they had brought tragedy as well as triumph. But the smile was the same—the soft voice, the slow gait, the quick gaze that sought to disguise its own penetration—there was no change here. But he was tired and looked it. He did not complain but asked eagerly about our boyhood friends, recalling incidents and sayings and little funny things as if they had happened yesterday. Of his own achievement he spoke deprecatingly. No man of equal distinction ever lived who shunned laudation and publicity more than O. Henry. He enjoyed his art in exact proportion as it received his own inner commendation. "Write to please yourself," he said. Do not be swerved by the presupposed tastes or expectations of any magazine or newspaper or reading public. The advice has been called worthless, but it is the only advice that genius, if true to itself, can give.

He kept to the last a gentleness, a sympathy, a cleanness of bearing, a reverence for womanhood, and an equal reverence for childhood that bespoke a nature ineradicably pure and wholesome. He was never even remotely effeminate, but there was much about him that one associates with healthy boyhood and unspoiled girlhood. One of his critics complains because O. Henry "slaps his reader on the back and laughs loudly as if in a barroom." O. Henry probably never in his life slapped anyone on the back or laughed boisterously. To see these traits in his writings you must contribute them yourself. The briefest acquaintance with him as boy or man would have convinced the critic that he might as well ascribe roystering to Dante or rowdyism to Whittier as to lay them at O. Henry's door. Is it possible that other readers so misinterpret the man from his works?

I do not believe that anyone ever came to know him in Greensboro, Texas, Columbus, or New York, who did not find love taking precedence of mere admiration. He was certainly the best loved boy in Greensboro, and all the interviews that I have had with those who were thrown intimately with him in later years tell the same story. Snobbishness he detected instantly and despised, for in every fiber of his being he was a democrat, a lover of his kind, especially of those seemingly down and out. A woman in New York said that she had almost despaired of making a living by her pen when, to her great surprise, O. Henry's card was brought in. She had never seen him, but had worshiped at a distance. He had heard of her plight, had learned that her stories had been rejected as regularly as they had been submitted, and had called to talk matters over. "This story is not at all bad," he said, when she had been prevailed upon to let him see her latest offering. "It's excellent. Let me suggest a change, a few minor changes, here and there." The story as thus modified was sent again on its rounds and a check for $750 was the immediate response. He loved to do things of this sort even when he had not a dollar in his pocket.

No story that he ever composed brings him back so vividly to me as do the lines that he wrote about himself to a stranger: "I was born and raised in 'No'th Ca'llina' and at eighteen went to Texas and ran wild on the prairies. Wild yet, but not so wild. Can't get to loving New Yorkers. Live all alone in a great big two rooms on quiet old Irving Place three doors from Wash. Irving's old home. Kind of lonesome. Was thinking lately (since the April moon commenced to shine) how I'd like to be down South, where I could happen over to Miss Ethel's or Miss Sallie's and sit down on the porch—not on a chair —on the edge of the porch, and lay my straw hat on the steps and lay my head back against the honeysuckle on the post—and just talk. And Miss Ethel would go in directly (they say 'presently' up here) and bring out the guitar. She would complain that the E string was broken, but no one would believe her; and pretty soon all of us would be singing the 'Swanee River' and 'In the Evening by the Moonlight' and—oh, gol darn it, what's the use of wishing?"

That is Will Porter as we knew him and loved him. It is O. Henry, too. But one note is lacking. We knew that in the Greensboro days childhood and womanhood evoked all the knightliness of his nature. But we did not know and the world did not know that, through all the sequent years of struggle and testing, the heart of a child and the heart of a woman had been the court of final appeal to which he had silently but resolutely shaped the issues of his life. He has told us in a few stanzas found on his desk when he died. He called his lines *The Crucible*. In the technique of his life, this bit of unexpected poetry is the surprise at the end. But, as in the endings of his stories, recognition takes precedence of surprise, recognition of a personality that kept faith with itself and from morning song to evening song held high the banner of a pure and potent idealism.

Hard ye may be in the tumult,
Red to your battle hilts,
Blow give for blow in the foray,
Cunningly ride in the tilts;
But when the roaring is ended,
Tenderly, unbeguiled,
Turn to a woman a woman's
Heart, and a child's to a child.

Test of the man if his worth be
In accord with the ultimate plan,
That he be not to his marring,
Always and utterly man;
That he bring out of the tumult,
Fitter and undefiled,
To a woman the heart of a woman,
To children the heart of a child.

Good when the bugles are ranting
It is to be iron and fire;
Good to be oak in the foray,
Ice to a guilty desire.
But when the battle is over
(Marvel and wonder the while)
Give to a woman a woman's
Heart, and a child's to a child.

C. Alphonso Smith

BIBLIOGRAPHY

Cabbages and Kings, 1904.
The Four Million, 1906.
The Trimmed Lamp, 1907.
Heart of the West, 1907.
The Voice of the City, 1908.
The Gentle Grafter, 1908.
Roads of Destiny, 1909.
Options, 1909.
Strictly Business, 1910.
Whirligigs, 1910.
Sixes and Sevens, 1911.
Rolling Stones, 1913.
Waifs and Strays, 1919.
Options is published by Harper and Brothers. The other volumes and also the O. Henry Biography, 1916, by the author of this sketch, are published by Doubleday, Page and Company, Garden City, New York.

TWO RENEGADES

From *Roads of Destiny*. Copyright, 1909, by Doubleday, Page and Company. By permission. The story appeared first in *Everybody's Magazine*, August, 1904.

IN the Gate City of the South the Confederate Veterans were reuniting; and I stood to see them march, beneath the tangled flags of the great conflict, to the hall of their oratory and commemoration.

While the irregular and halting line was passing I made onslaught upon it and dragged forth from the ranks my friend Barnard O'Keefe, who had no right to be there. For he was a Northerner born and bred; and what should he be doing hallooing for the Stars and Bars among those gray and moribund veterans? And why should he be trudging, with his shining, martial, humorous, broad face, among those warriors of a previous and alien generation?

I say I dragged him forth, and held him till the last hickory leg and waving goatee had stumbled past. And then I hustled him out of the crowd into a cool interior; for the Gate City was stirred that day, and the hand-organs wisely eliminated "Marching Through Georgia" from their repertories.

"Now, what deviltry are you up to?" I asked of O'Keefe when there were a table and things in glasses between us.

O'Keefe wiped his heated face and instigated a commotion among the floating ice in his glass before he chose to answer.

"I am assisting at the wake," said he, "of the only nation on earth that ever did me a good turn. As one gentleman to another, I am ratifying and celebrating the foreign policy of the late Jefferson Davis, as fine a statesman as ever settled the financial question of a barrel of money for a barrel of flour—a pair of $20 bills for a pair of boots—a hatful of currency for a new hat—say, ain't that simple compared with W. J. B.'s little old oxidized plank?"

"What talk is this?" I asked. "Your financial disgression

is merely a subterfuge. Why were you marching in the ranks of the Confederate Veterans?"

"Because, my lad," answered O'Keefe, "the Confederate Government in its might and power interposed to protect and defend Barnard O'Keefe against immediate and dangerous assassination at the hands of a blood-thirsty foreign country after the United States of America had overruled his appeal for protection, and had instructed Private Secretary Cortelyou to reduce his estimate of the Republican majority for 1905 by one vote."

"Come, Barney," said I, "the Confederate States of America has been out of existence nearly forty years. You do not look older yourself. When was it that the deceased government exerted its foreign policy in your behalf?"

"Four months ago," said O'Keefe promptly. "The infamous foreign power I alluded to is still staggering from the official blow dealt it by Mr. Davis's contraband aggregation of states. That's why you see me cake-walking with the ex-rebs to the illegitimate tune about ,'simmon-seeds and cotton. I vote for the Great Father in Washington, but I am not going back on Mars' Jeff. You say the Confederacy has been dead forty years? Well, if it hadn't been for it, I'd have been breathing to-day with soul so dead I couldn't have whispered a single cuss-word about my native land. The O'Keefes are not overburdened with ingratitude."

I must have looked bewildered. "The war was over," I said vacantly, "in——"

O'Keefe laughed loudly, scattering my thoughts.

"Ask old Doc Millikin if the war is over!" he shouted, hugely diverted. "Oh, no! Doc hasn't surrendered yet. And the Confederate States! Well, I just told you they bucked officially and solidly and nationally against a foreign government four months ago and kept me from being shot. Old Jeff's country stepped in and brought me off under its wing while Roosevelt was having a gunboat repainted and waiting for the National Campaign Committee to look up whether I had ever scratched the ticket."

"Isn't there a story in this, Barney?" I asked.

"No," said O'Keefe; "but I'll give you the facts. You know I went down to Panama when this irritation about a canal began. I thought I'd get in on the ground floor. I did, and had to sleep on it, and drink water with little zoos in it; so, of course, I got the chagres fever. That was in a little town called San Juan on the coast.

"After I got the fever hard enough to kill a Port-au-Prince nigger, I had a relapse in the shape of Doc Millikin.

"There was a doctor to attend a sick man! If Doc Millikin had your case, he made the terrors of death seem like an invitation to a donkey-party. He had the bedside manners of a Piute medicine-man and the soothing presence of a dray loaded with iron bridge-girders. When he laid his hand on your fevered brow you felt like Cap John Smith just before Pocahontas went his bail.

"Well, this old medical outrage floated down to my shack when I sent for him. He was built like a shad, and his eyebrows was black, and his white whiskers trickled down from his chin like milk coming out of a sprinkling-pot. He had a nigger boy along carrying an old tomato-can full of calomel, and a saw.

"Doc felt my pulse, and then he began to mess up some calomel with an agricultural implement that belonged to the trowel class.

" 'I don't want any death-mask made yet, Doc,' I says, 'nor my liver put in a plaster-of-Paris cast. I'm sick; and it's medicine I need, not frescoing.'

" 'You're a blame Yankee, ain't you?" asks Doc, going on mixing up his Portland cement.

"I'm from the North,' says I, 'but I'm a plain man, and don't care for mural decorations. When you get the Isthmus all asphalted over with that boll-weevil prescription, would you mind giving me a dose of pain-killer, or a little strychnine on toast to ease up this feeling of unhealthiness that I have got?'

" 'They was all sassy, just like you,' says old Doc, 'but

we lowered their temperature considerable. Yes, sir, I reckon
we sent a good many of ye over to old *mortuis nisi bonum.*
Look at Antietam and Bull Run and Seven Pines and around
Nashville! There never was a battle where we didn't lick
ye unless you was ten to our one. I knew you was a blame
Yankee the minute I laid eyes on you.'

" 'Don't re-open the chasm, Doc,' I begs him. "Any
Yankeeness I may have is geographical; and, as far as I am
concerned, a Southerner is as good as a Filipino any day.
I'm feeling too bad to argue. Let's have secession without
misrepresentation, if you say so; but what I need is more
laudanum and less Lundy's Lane. If you're mixing that
compound gefloxide of gefloxicum for me, please fill my ears
with it before you get around to the battle of Gettysburg,
for there is a subject full of talk.'

"By this time Doc Millikin had thrown up a line of forti-
fications on square pieces of paper; and he says to me: 'Yank,
take one of these powders every two hours. They won't kill
you. I'll be around again about sundown to see if you're
alive.'

"Old Doc's powders knocked the chagres. I stayed in
San Juan, and got to knowing him better. He was from
Mississippi, and the red-hottest Southerner that ever smelled
mint. He made Stonewall Jackson and R. E. Lee look like
Abolitionists. He had a family somewhere down near Yazoo
City; but he stayed away from the States on account of an
uncontrollable liking he had for the absence of a Yankee
government. Him and me got as thick personally as the
Emperor of Russia and the dove of peace, but sectionally
we didn't amalgamate.

" 'Twas a beautiful system of medical practice introduced
by old Doc into that isthmus of land. He'd take that bracket-
saw and the mild chloride and his hypodermic, and treat anything from yellow fever to a personal friend.

"Besides his other liabilities Doc could play a flute for a
minute or two. He was guilty of two tunes—'Dixie' and
another one that was mighty close to the 'Suwanee River'—

you might say one of its tributaries. He used to come down and sit with me while I was getting well, and aggrieve his flute and say unreconstructed things about the North. You'd have thought the smoke from the first gun at Fort Sumter was still floating around in the air.

"You know that was about the time they staged them property revolutions down there, that wound up in the fifth act with the thrilling canal scene where Uncle Sam has nine curtain-calls holding Miss Panama by the hand, while the bloodhounds keep Senator Morgan treed up in a cocoanut-palm.

"That's the way it wound up; but at first it seemed as if Colombia was going to make Panama look like one of the $3.98 kind, with dents made in it in the factory, like they wear at North Beach fish fries. For mine, I played the straw-hat crowd to win; and they gave me a colonel's commission over a brigade of twenty-seven men in the left wing and second joint of the insurgent army.

"The Colombian troops were awfully rude to us. One day when I had my brigade in a sandy spot, with its shoes off doing a battalion drill by squads, the Government army rushed from behind a bush at us, acting as noisy and disagreeable as they could.

"My troops enfiladed, left-faced, and left the spot. After enticing the enemy for three miles or so we struck a brier-patch and had to sit down. When we were ordered to throw up our toes and surrender we obeyed. Five of my best staff-officers fell, suffering extremely with stone-bruised heels.

"Then and there those Colombians took your friend Barney, sir, stripped him of the insignia of his rank, consisting of a pair of brass knuckles and a canteen of rum, and dragged him before a military court. The presiding general went through the usual legal formalities that sometimes cause a case to hang on the calendar of a South American military court as long as ten minutes. He asked me my age, and then sentenced me to be shot.

"They woke up the court interpreter, an American named

Jenks, who was in the rum business and vice versa, and told
him to translate the verdict.

"Jenks stretched himself and took a morphine tablet.

" 'You've got to back up against th' 'dobe, old man,' says
he to me. 'Three weeks, I believe, you get. Haven't got
a chew of fine-cut on you, have you?'

" 'Translate that again, with foot-notes and a glossary,'
says I. 'I don't know whether I'm discharged, condemned,
or handed over to the Gerry Society.'

" 'Oh,' says Jenks, 'don't you understand? You're to
be stood up against a 'dobe wall and shot in two or three
weeks—three, I think, they said.'

" 'Would you mind asking 'em which?' says I. 'A week
don't amount to much after you are dead, but it seems a real
nice long spell while you are alive.'

" 'It's two weeks,' says the interpreter, after inquiring
in Spanish of the court. 'Shall I ask 'em again?'

" 'Let be,' says I. 'Let's have a stationary verdict. If
I keep on appealing this way they'll have me shot about ten
days before I was captured. No, I haven't got any fine-cut.'

"They sends me over to the *calaboza* with a detachment
of coloured postal-telegraph boys carrying Enfield rifles, and
I am locked up in a kind of brick bakery. The temperature
in there was just about the kind mentioned in the cooking
recipes that call for a quick oven.

"Then I gives a silver dollar to one of the guards to send
for the United States consul. He comes around in pajamas,
with a pair of glasses on his nose and a dozen or two inside
of him.

" 'I'm to be shot in two weeks,' says I. 'And although
I've made a memorandum of it, I don't seem to get it off my
mind. You want to call up Uncle Sam on the cable as quick
as you can and get him all worked up about it. Have 'em
send the *Kentucky* and the *Kearsarge* and the *Oregon* down
right away. That'll be about enough battleships; but it
wouldn't hurt to have a couple of cruisers and a torpedo-boat

destroyer, too. And—say, if Dewey isn't busy, better have him come along on the fastest one of the fleet.'

" 'Now, see here, O'Keefe,' says the consul, getting the best of a hiccup, 'what do you want to bother the State Department about this matter for?'

" 'Didn't you hear me?' says I; 'I'm to be shot in two weeks. Did you think I said I was going to a lawn-party? And it wouldn't hurt if Roosevelt could get the Japs to send down the *Yellowyamtiskookum* or the *Ogotosingsing* or some other first-class cruisers to help. It would make me feel safer.'

" 'Now, what you want,' says the consul, 'is not to get excited. I'll send you over some chewing tobacco and some banana fritters when I go back. The United States can't interfere in this. You know you were caught insurging against the government, and you're subject to the laws of this country. Tell you the truth, I've had an intimation from the State Department—unofficially, of course—that whenever a soldier of fortune demands a fleet of gunboats in a case of revolutionary *katzenjammer*, I should cut the cable, give him all the tobacco he wants, and after he's shot take his clothes, if they fit me, for part payment of my salary.'

" 'Consul,' says I to him, 'this is a serious question. You are representing Uncle Sam. This ain't any little international tomfoolery, like a universal peace congress or the christening of the *Shamrock IV*. I'm an American citizen and I demand protection. I demand the Mosquito fleet, and Schley, and the Atlantic squadron, and Bob Evans, and General E. Byrd Grubb, and two or three protocols. What are you going to do about it?'

" 'Nothing doing,' says the consul.

" 'Be off with you, then,' says I, out of patience with him, 'and send me Doc Millikin. Ask Doc to come and see me.'

"Doc comes and looks through the bars at me, surrounded by dirty soldiers, with even my shoes and canteen confiscated, and he looks mightily pleased.

" 'Hello, Yank,' says he, 'getting a little taste of Johnson's Island, now, ain't ye?'

" 'Doc,' says I, 'I've just had an interview with the U. S. consul. I gather from his remarks that I might just as well have been caught selling suspenders in Kishineff under the name of Rosenstein as to be in my present condition. It seems that the only maritime aid I am to receive from the United States is some navy-plug to chew. Doc,' says I, 'can't you suspend hostilities on the slavery question long enough to do something for me?'

" 'It ain't been my habit,' Doc Millikin answers, 'to do any painless dentistry when I find a Yank cutting an eye-tooth. So the Stars and Stripes ain't landing any marines to shell the huts of the Colombian cannibals, hey? Oh, say, can you see by the dawn's early light the star-spangled banner has fluked in the fight? What's the matter with the War Department, hey? It's a great thing to be a citizen of a gold-standard nation, aint' it?'

" 'Rub it in, Doc, all you want,' says I. 'I guess we're weak on foreign policy.'

" 'For a Yank,' says Doc, putting on his specs and talking more mild, 'you ain't so bad. If you had come from below the line I reckon I would have liked you right smart. Now since your country has gone back on you, you have to come to the old doctor whose cotton you burned and whose mules you stole and whose niggers you freed to help you. Ain't that so, Yank?'

" 'It is,' says I heartily, 'and let's have a diagnosis of the case right away, for in two weeks' time all you can do is to hold an autopsy and I don't want to be amputated if I can help it.'

" 'Now,' says Doc, business-like, 'it's easy enough for you to get out of this scrape. Money'll do it. You've got to pay a long string of 'em from General Pomposo down to this anthropoid ape guarding your door. About $10,000 will do the trick. Have you got the money?'

" 'Me?' says I. 'I've got one Chili dollar, two *real* pieces, and a *medio.*'

" 'Then if you've any last words, utter 'em,' says that old reb. 'The roster of your financial budget sounds quite much to me like the noise of a requiem.'

" 'Change the treatment,' says I. 'I admit that I'm short. Call a consultation or use radium or smuggle me in some saws or something.'

" 'Yank,' says Doc Millikin, 'I've a good notion to help you. There's only one government in the world that can get you out of this difficulty; and that's the Confederate States of America, the grandest nation that ever existed.'

"Just as you said to me I says to Doc: 'Why, the Confederacy ain't a nation. It's been absolved forty years ago.'

" 'That's a campaign lie,' says Doc. 'She's running along as solid as the Roman Empire. She's the only hope you've got. Now, you, being a Yank, have got to go through with some preliminary obsequies before you can get official aid. You've got to take the oath of allegiance to the Confederate Government. Then I'll guarantee she does all she can for you. What do you say, Yank?—it's your last chance.'

" 'If you're fooling with me, Doc,' I answers, 'you're no better than the United States. But as you say it's the last chance, hurry up and swear me. I always did like corn whisky and 'possum anyhow. I believe I'm half Southerner by nature. I'm willing to try the Ku-Klux in place of the khaki. Get brisk.'

"Doc Millikin thinks awhile, and then he offers me this oath of allegiance to take without any kind of a chaser:

" 'I, Barnard O'Keefe, Yank, being of sound body but a Republican mind, hereby swear to transfer my fealty, respect, and allegiance to the Confederate States of America, and the government thereof in consideration of said government, through its official acts and powers, obtaining my freedom and release from confinement and sentence of death brought about by the exuberance of my Irish proclivities and my general pizenness as a Yank.'

"I repeated these words after Doc, but they seemed to me a kind of hocus-pocus; and I don't believe any life-insurance company in the country would have issued me a policy on the strength of 'em.

"Doc went away saying he would communicate with his government immediately.

"Say—you can imagine how I felt—me to be shot in two weeks and my only hope for help being in a government that's been dead so long that it isn't even remembered except on Decoration Day and when Joe Wheeler signs the voucher for his pay-check. But it was all there was in sight; and somehow I thought Doc Millikin had something up his old alpaca sleeve that wasn't all foolishness.

"Around to the jail comes old Doc again in about a week. I was flea-bitten, a mite sarcastic, and fundamentally hungry.

" 'Any Confederate ironclads in the offing?' I asks 'Do you notice any sounds resembling the approach of Jeb Stewart's cavalry overland or Stonewall Jackson sneaking up in the rear? If you do, I wish you'd say so.'

" 'It's too soon yet for help to come,' says Doc.

" 'The sooner the better,' says I. 'I don't care if it gets in fully fifteen minutes before I am shot; and if you happen to lay eyes on Beauregard or Albert Sidney Johnston or any of the relief corps, wig-wag 'em to hike along.'

" 'There's been no answer received yet,' says Doc.

" 'Don't forget,' says I, 'that there's only four days more. I don't know how you propose to work this thing, Doc,' I says to him; 'but it seems to me I'd sleep better if you had got a government that was alive and on the map—like Afghanistan or Great Britain, or old man Kruger's kingdom, to take this matter up. I don't mean any disrespect to your Confederate States, but I can't help feeling that my chances of being pulled out of this scrape was decidedly weakened when General Lee surrendered.'

" 'It's your only chance,' said Doc; 'don't quarrel with it. What did your own country do for you?'

"It was only two days before the morning I was to be shot, when Doc Milliken came around again.

" 'All right, Yank,' says he. 'Help's come. The Confederate States of America is going to apply for your release. The representatives of the government arrived on a fruit-steamer last night.'

" 'Bully!' says I—'bully for you, Doc! I suppose it's marines with a Gatling. I'm going to love your country all I can for this.'

" 'Negotiations,' says old Doc, 'will be opened between the two governments at once. You will know later on to-day if they are successful.'

"About four in the afternoon a soldier in red trousers brings a paper round to the jail, and they unlocks the door and I walks out. The guard at the door bows and I bows, and I steps into the grass and wades around to Doc Millikin's shack.

"Doc was sitting in his hammock playing 'Dixie,' soft and low and out of tune, on his flute. I interrupted him at 'Look away! look away!' and shook his hand for five minutes.

" 'I never thought,' says Doc, taking a chew fretfully, 'that I'd ever try to save any blame Yank's life. But, Mr. O'Keefe, I don't see but what you are entitled to be considered part human, anyhow. I never thought Yanks had any of the rudiments of decorum and laudability about them. I reckon I might have been too aggregative in my tabulation. But it ain't me you want to thank—it's the Confederate States of America.'

" 'And I'm much obliged to 'em,' says I. 'It's a poor man that wouldn't be patriotic with a country that's saved his life. I'll drink to the Stars and Bars whenever there's a flag-staff and a glass convenient. But where,' says I, 'are the rescuing troops? If there was a gun fired or a shell burst, I didn't hear it.'

"Doc Millikin raises up and points out the window with his flute at the banana-steamer loading with fruit.

" 'Yank,' says he, 'there's a steamer that's going to sail

in the morning. If I was you, I'd sail on it. The Confederate Government's done all it can for you. There wasn't a gun fired. The negotiations was carried on secretly between the two nations by the purser of that steamer. I got him to do it because I didn't want to appear in it. Twelve thousand dollars was paid to the officials in bribes to let you go.'

" 'Man!' says I, sitting down hard—'twelve thousand—how will I ever—who could have—where did the money come from?'

" 'Yazoo City,' says Doc Millikin; 'I've got a little saved up there. Two barrels full. It looks good to these Colombians. 'Twas Confederate money, every dollar of it. Now do you see why you'd better leave before they try to pass some of it on an expert?'

" 'I do,' says I.

" 'Now let's hear you give the password,' says Doc Millikin.

" 'Hurrah for Jeff Davis!' says I.

" 'Correct,' says Doc. 'And let me tell you something: The next tune I learn on my flute is going to be "Yankee Doodle." I reckon there's some Yanks that are not so pizen. Or, if you was me, would you try "The Red, White, and Blue"?' "

AN UNFINISHED STORY

From *The Four Million*. Copyright, 1906, by Doubleday, Page and Company. By permission. First published in *McClure's Magazine*, August, 1905.

We no longer groan and heap ashes upon our heads when the flames of Tophet are mentioned. For even the preachers have begun to tell us that God is radium, or ether or some scientific compound, and that the worst we wicked ones may expect is a chemical reaction. This is a pleasing hypothesis; but there lingers yet some of the old, goodly terror of orthodoxy.

There are but two subjects upon which one may discourse

with a free imagination, and without the possibility of being controverted. You may talk of your dreams; and you may tell what you heard a parrot say. Both Morpheus and the bird are incompetent witnesses; and your listener dare not attack your recital. The baseless fabric of a vision, then, shall furnish my theme—chosen with apologies and regrets— instead of the more limited field of pretty Polly's small talk.

I had a dream that was so far removed from the higher criticism that it had to do with the ancient, respectable, and lamented bar-of-judgment theory.

Gabriel had played his trump; and those of us who could not follow suit were arraigned for examination. I noticed at one side a gathering of professional bondsmen in solemn black and collars that buttoned behind; but it seemed there was some trouble about their real estate titles; and they did not appear to be getting any of us out.

A fly cop—an angel policeman—flew over to me and took me by the left wing. Near at hand was a group of very prosperous-looking spirits arraigned for judgment.

"Do you belong with that bunch?" the policeman asked.

"Who are they?" was my answer.

"Why," said he, "they are—"

But this irrevelant stuff is taking up space that the story should occupy.

Dulcie worked in a department store. She sold Hamburg edging, or stuffed peppers, or automobiles, or other little trinkets such as they keep in department stores. Of what she earned, Dulcie received six dollars per week. The remainder was credited to her and debited to somebody else's account in the ledger kept by G—— Oh, primal energy, you say, Reverend Doctor— Well then, in the Ledger of Primal Energy.

During her first year in the store, Dulcie was paid five dollars per week. It would be instructive to know how she lived on that amount. Don't care? Very well; probably you are interested in larger amounts. Six dollars is a larger amount. I will tell you how she lived on six dollars per week.

One afternoon at six, when Dulcie was sticking her hatpin within an eighth of an inch of her *medulla oblongata*, she said to her chum, Sadie—the girl that waits on you with her left side:

"Say, Sade, I made a date for dinner this evening with Piggy."

"You never did!" exclaimed Sadie admiringly. "Well, ain't you the lucky one? Piggy's an awful swell; and he always takes a girl to swell places. He took Blanche up to the Hoffman House one evening, where they have swell music, and you see a lot of swells. You'll have a swell time, Dulce."

Dulcie hurried homeward. Her eyes were shining, and her cheeks showed the delicate pink of life's—real life's—approaching dawn. It was Friday; and she had fifty cents left of her last week's wages.

The streets were filled with the rush-hour floods of people. The electric lights of Broadway were glowing—calling moths from miles, from leagues, from hundreds of leagues out of darkness around to come in and attend the singeing school. Men in accurate clothes, with faces like those carved on cherry stones by the old salts in sailors' homes, turned and stared at Dulcie as she sped, unheeding, past them. Manhattan, the night-blooming cereus, was beginning to unfold its dead-white, heavy-odoured petals.

Dulcie stopped in a store where goods were cheap and bought an imitation lace collar with her fifty cents. That money was to have been spent otherwise—fifteen cents for supper, ten cents for breakfast, ten cents for lunch. Another dime was to be added to her small store of savings; and five cents was to be squandered for licorice drops—the kind that made your cheek look like the toothache, and last as long. The licorice was an extravagance—almost a carouse—but what is life without pleasures?

Dulcie lived in a furnished room. There is this difference

between a furnished room and a boarding-house. In a furnished room, other people do not know it when you go hungry.

Dulcie went up to her room—the third floor back in a West Side brownstone front. She lit the gas. Scientists tell us that the diamond is the hardest substance known. Their mistake. Landladies know of a compound beside which the diamond is as putty. They pack it in the tips of gas-burners; and one may stand on a chair and dig at it in vain until one's fingers are pink and bruised. A hairpin will not remove it; therefore let us call it immovable.

So Dulcie lit the gas. In its one-fourth-candle-power glow we will observe the room.

Couch-bed, dresser, table, washstand, chair—of this much the landlady was guilty. The rest was Dulcie's. On the dresser were her treasures—a gilt china vase presented to her by Sadie, a calendar issued by a pickle works, a book on the divination of dreams, some rice powder in a glass dish, and a cluster of artificial cherries tied with a pink ribbon.

Against the wrinkly mirror stood pictures of General Kitchener, William Muldoon, the Duchess of Marlborough, and Benvenuto Cellini. Against one wall was a plaster of Paris plaque of an O'Callahan in a Roman helmet. Near it was a violent oleograph of a lemon-coloured child assaulting an inflammatory butterfly. This was Dulcie's final judgment in art; but it had never been upset. Her rest had never been disturbed by whispers of stolen copes; no critic had elevated his eyebrows at her infantile entomologist.

Piggy was to call for her at seven. While she swiftly makes ready, let us discretely face the other way and gossip.

For the room, Dulcie paid two dollars per week. On week-days her breakfast cost ten cents; she made coffee and cooked an egg over the gaslight while she was dressing. On Sunday mornings she feasted royally on veal chops and pineapple fritters at "Billy's" restaurant, at a cost of twenty-five cents—and tipped the waitress ten cents. New York presents so many temptations for one to run into extravagance.

She had her lunches in the department-store restaurant at a cost of sixty cents for the week; dinners were $1.05. The evening papers—show me a New Yorker going without his daily paper!—came to six cents; and two Sunday papers— one for the personal column and the other to read—were ten cents. The total amounts to $4.76. Now, one has to buy clothes, and—

I give it up. I hear of wonderful bargains in fabrics, and of miracles performed with needle and thread; but I am in doubt. I hold my pen poised in vain when I would add to Dulcie's life some of those joys that belong to woman by virtue of all the unwritten, sacred, natural, inactive or- dinances of the equity of heaven. Twice she had been to Coney Island and had ridden the hobby-horses. 'Tis a weary thing to count your pleasures by summers instead of by hours.

Piggy needs but a word. When the girls named him, an undeserving stigma was cast upon the noble family of swine. The words-of-three-letters lesson in the old blue spelling book begins with Piggy's biography. He was fat; he had the soul of a rat, the habits of a bat, and the magnanimity of a cat. . . . He wore expensive clothes; and was a con- noisseur in starvation. He could look at a shop-girl and tell you to an hour how long it had been since she had eaten anything more nourishing than marshmallows and tea. He hung about the shopping districts, and prowled around in department stores with his invitations to dinner. Men who escort dogs upon the streets at the end of a string look down upon him. He is a type; I can dwell upon him no longer; my pen is not the kind intended for him; I am no carpenter.

At ten minutes to seven Dulcie was ready. She looked at herself in the wrinkly mirror. The reflection was satis- factory. The dark blue dress, fitting without a wrinkle, the hat with its jaunty black feather, the but-slightly-soiled gloves —all representing self-denial, even of food itself—were vastly becoming.

Dulcie forgot everything else for a moment except that she was beautiful, and that life was about to lift a corner

of its mysterious veil for her to observe its wonders. No
gentleman had ever asked her out before. Now she was
going for a brief moment into the glitter and exalted show.

The girls said that Piggy was a "spender." There would
be a grand dinner, and music, and splendidly dressed ladies
to look at, and things to eat that strangely twisted the girls'
jaws when they tried to tell about them. No doubt she would
be asked out again.

There was a blue pongee suit in a window that she knew
—by saving twenty cents a week instead of ten, in—let's see
—Oh, it would run into years! But there was a second-
hand store in Seventh Avenue where—

Somebody knocked at the door. Dulcie opened it. The
landlady stood there with a spurious smile, sniffing for cooking by stolen gas.

"A gentleman's downstairs to see you," she said. "Name
is Mr. Wiggins."

By such epithet was Piggy known to unfortunate ones
who had to take him seriously.

Dulcie turned to the dresser to get her handkerchief; and
then she stopped still, and bit her under lip hard. While
looking in her mirror she had seen fairyland and herself, a
princess, just awakening from a long slumber. She had for-
gotten one that was watching her with sad, beautiful, stern
eyes—the only one there was to approve or condemn what
she did. Straight and slender and tall, with a look of sorrow-
ful reproach on his handsome, melancholy face, General
Kitchener fixed his wonderful eyes on her out of his gilt
photograph frame on the dresser.

Dulcie turned like an automatic doll to the landlady.

"Tell him I can't go," she said dully. "Tell him I'm
sick, or something. Tell him I'm not going out."

After the door was closed and locked, Dulcie fell upon
her bed, crushing her black tip, and cried for ten minutes.
General Kitchener was her only friend. He was Dulcie's
ideal of a gallant knight. He looked as if he might have a
secret sorrow, and his wonderful moustache was a dream,

and she was a little afraid of that stern yet tender look in his eyes. She used to have little fancies that he would call at the house sometime, and ask for her, with his sword clanking against his high boots. Once, when a boy was rattling a piece of chain against a lamp-post she had opened the window and looked out. But there was no use. She knew that General Kitchener was away over in Japan, leading his army against the savage Turks; and he would never step out of his gilt frame for her. Yet one look from him had vanquished Piggy that night. Yes, for that night.

When her cry was over Dulcie got up and took off her best dress, and put on her old blue kimono. She wanted no dinner. She sang two verses of "Sammy." Then she became intensely interested in a little red speck on the side of her nose. And after that was attended to, she drew up a chair to the rickety table, and told her fortune with an old deck of cards.

"The horrid, impudent thing!" she said aloud. "And I never gave him a word or a look to make him think it!"

At nine o'clock Dulcie took a tin box of crackers and a little pot of raspberry jam out of her trunk, and had a feast. She offered General Kitchener some jam on a cracker; but he only looked at her as the sphinx would have looked at a butterfly—if there are butterflies in the desert,

"Don't eat it if you don't want to," said Dulcie. "And don't put on so many airs and scold so with your eyes. I wonder if you'd be so superior and snippy if you had to live on six dollars a week."

It was not a good sign for Dulcie to be rude to General Kitchener. And then she turned Benvenuto Cellini's face downward with a severe gesture. But that was not inexcusable; for she had always thought he was Henry VIII, and she did not approve of him.

At half-past nine Dulcie took a last look at the pictures on the dresser, turned out the light, and skipped into bed. It's an awful thing to go to bed with a good-night look at

General Kitchener, William Muldoon, the Duchess of Marlborough, and Benvenuto Cellini.

This story really doesn't get anywhere at all. The rest
of it comes later—sometime when Piggy asks Dulcie again
to dine with him, and she is feeling lonelier than usual, and
General Kitchener happens to be looking the other way; and
then—

As I said before, I dreamed that I was standing near a
crowd of prosperous-looking angels, and a policeman took
me by the wing and asked if I belonged with them.

"Who are they?" I asked.

"Why," said he, "they are the men who hired working-
girls, and paid 'em five or six dollars a week to live on. Are
you one of the bunch?"

"Not on your immortality," said I. "I'm only the fellow
that set fire to an orphan asylum, and murdered a blind
man for his pennies."

THE GIFT OF THE MAGI

From *The Four Million.* Copyright, 1906, by Doubleday, Page and Company. By
permission. First published in *The World*, New York, December 10, 1905.

ONE dollar and eighty-seven cents. That was all. And
sixty cents of it was in pennies. Pennies saved one and two
at a time by bulldozing the grocer and the vegetable man
and the butcher until one's cheeks burned with the silent
imputation of parsimony that such close dealing implied.
Three times Della counted it. One dollar and eighty-seven
cents. And the next day would be Christmas.

There was clearly nothing to do but flop down on the
shabby little couch and howl. So Della did it. Which in-
stigates the moral reflection that life is made up of sobs,
sniffles, and smiles, with sniffles predominating.

While the mistress of the home is gradually subsiding
from the first stage to the second, take a look at the home.

A furnished flat at $8 per week. It did not exactly beggar description, but it certainly had that word on the lookout for the mendicancy squad.

In the vestibule below was a letter-box into which no letter would go, and an electric button from which no mortal finger could coax a ring. Also appertaining thereunto was a card bearing the name "Mr. James Dillingham Young."

The "Dillingham" had been flung to the breeze during a former period of prosperity when its possessor was being paid $30 per week. Now, when the income was shrunk to $20, the letters of "Dillingham" looked blurred, as though they were thinking seriously of contracting to a modest and unassuming D. But whenever Mr. James Dillingham Young came home and reached his flat above he was called "Jim" and greatly hugged by Mrs. James Dillingham Young, already introduced to you as Della. Which is all very good.

Della finished her cry and attended to her cheeks with the powder rag. She stood by the window and looked out dully at a grey cat walking a grey fence in a grey backyard. To-morrow would be Christmas Day, and she had only $1.87 with which to buy Jim a present. She had been saving every penny she could for months, with this result. Twenty dollars a week doesn't go far. Expenses had been greater than she had calculated. They always are. Only $1.87 to buy a present for Jim. Her Jim. Many a happy hour she had spent planning for something nice for him. Something fine and rare and sterling—something just a little bit near to being worthy of the honour of being owned by Jim.

There was a pier-glass between the windows of the room. Perhaps you have seen a pier-glass in an $8 flat. A very thin and very agile person may, by observing his reflection in a rapid sequence of longitudinal strips, obtain a fairly accurate conception of his looks. Della, being slender, had mastered the art.

Suddenly she whirled from the window and stood before the glass. Her eyes were shining brilliantly, but her face had lost its colour within twenty seconds. Rapidly she pulled down her hair and let it fall to its full length.

Now, there were two possessions of the James Dillingham Youngs in which they both took a mighty pride. One was Jim's gold watch that had been his father's and his grandfather's. The other was Della's hair. Had the Queen of Sheba lived in the flat across the airshaft, Della would have let her hair hang out the window some day to dry just to depreciate Her Majesty's jewels and gifts. Had King Solomon been the janitor, with all his treasures piled up in the basement, Jim would have pulled out his watch every time he passed, just to see him pluck at his beard from envy.

So now Della's beautiful hair fell about her, rippling and shining like a cascade of brown waters. It reached below her knee and made itself almost a garment for her. And then she did it up again nervously and quickly. Once she faltered for a minute and stood still while a tear or two splashed on the worn red carpet.

On went her old brown jacket; on went her old brown hat. With a whirl of skirts and with the brilliant sparkle still in her eyes, she fluttered out the door and down the stairs to the street.

Where she stopped the sign read: "Mme. Sofronie. Hair Goods of All Kinds." One flight up Della ran, and collected herself, panting. Madame, large, too white, chilly, hardly looked the "Sofronie."

"Will you buy my hair?" asked Della.

"I buy hair," said Madame. "Take yer hat off and let's have a sight at the looks of it."

Down rippled the brown cascade.

"Twenty dollars," said Madame, lifting the mass with a practiced hand.

"Give it to me quick," said Della.

Oh, and the next two hours tripped by on rosy wings. Forget the hashed metaphor. She was ransacking the stores for Jim's present.

She found it at last. It surely had been made for Jim

and no one else. There was no other like it in any of the
stores, and she had turned all of them inside out. It was a
platinum fob chain simple and chaste in design, properly pro-
claiming its value by substance alone and not by meretricious
ornamentation—as all good things should do. It was even
worthy of The Watch. As soon as she saw it she knew that
it must be Jim's. It was like him. Quietness and value—
the description applied to both. Twenty-one dollars they took
from her for it, and she hurried home with the 87 cents.
With that chain on his watch Jim might be properly anxious
about the time in any company. Grand as the watch was, he
sometimes looked at it on the sly on account of the old leather
strap that he used in place of a chain.

When Della reached home her intoxication gave way
a little to prudence and reason. She got out her curling irons
and lighted the gas and went to work repairing the ravages
made by generosity added to love. Which is always a tre-
mendous task, dear friends—a mammoth task.

Within forty minutes her head was covered with tiny,
close-lying curls that made her look wonderfully like a truant
schoolboy. She looked at her reflection in the mirror long,
carefully, and critically.

"If Jim doesn't kill me," she said to herself, "before he
takes a second look at me, he'll say I look like a Coney Island
chorus girl. But what could I do—oh! what could I do
with a dollar and eighty-seven cents?"

At 7 o'clock the coffee was made and the frying-pan was
on the back of the stove hot and ready to cook the chops.

Jim was never late. Della doubled the fob chain in her
hand and sat on the corner of the table near the door that
he always entered. Then she heard his step on the stair
away down on the first flight, and she turned white for just
a moment. She had a habit of saying little silent prayers
about the simplest everyday things, and now she whispered:
"Please God, make him think I am still pretty."

The door opened and Jim stepped in and closed it. He
looked thin and very serious. Poor fellow, he was only

twenty-two—and to be burdened with a family! He needed a new overcoat and he was without gloves.

Jim stopped inside the door, as immovable as a setter at the scent of quail. His eyes were fixed upon Della, and there was an expression in them that she could not read, and it terrified her. It was not anger, nor surprise, nor disapproval, nor horror, nor any of the sentiments that she had been prepared for. He simply stared at her fixedly with that peculiar expression on his face.

Della wriggled off the table and went for him.

"Jim, darling," she cried, "don't look at me that way. I had my hair cut off and sold it because I couldn't have lived through Christmas without giving you a present. It'll grow out again—you won't mind, will you? I just had to do it. My hair grows awfully fast. Say 'Merry Christmas!' Jim, and let's be happy. You don't know what a nice—what a beautiful, nice gift I've got for you."

"You've cut off your hair?" asked Jim, laboriously, as if he had not arrived at that patent fact yet even after the hardest mental labour.

"Cut it off and sold it," said Della. "Don't you like me just as well, anyhow? I'm me without my hair, ain't I?"

Jim looked about the room curiously.

"You say your hair is gone?" he said, with an air almost of idiocy.

"You needn't look for it," said Della. "It's sold, I tell you—sold and gone, too. It's Christmas Eve, boy. Be good to me, for it went for you. Maybe the hairs of my head were numbered," she went on with a sudden serious sweetness, "but nobody could ever count my love for you. Shall I put the chops on, Jim?"

Out of his trance Jim seemed quickly to wake. He enfolded his Della. For ten seconds let us regard with discreet scrutiny some inconsequential object in the other direction. Eight dollars a week or a million a year—what is the difference? A mathematician or a wit would give you the wrong answer. The magi brought valuable gifts, but that was not among them. This dark assertion will be illuminated later on.

Jim drew a package from his overcoat pocket and threw it upon the table.

"Don't make any mistake, Dell," he said, "about me. I don't think there's anything in the way of a haircut or a shave or a shampoo that could make me like my girl any less. But if you'll unwrap that package you may see why you had me going a while at first."

White fingers and nimble tore at the string and paper. And then an ecstatic scream of joy; and then, alas! a quick feminine change to hysterical tears and wails, necessitating the immediate employment of all the comforting powers of the lord of the flat.

For there lay The Combs—the set of combs, side and back, that Della had worshipped for long in a Broadway window. Beautiful combs, pure tortoise shell, with jeweled rims—just the shade to wear in the beautiful vanished hair. They were expensive combs, she knew, and her heart had simply craved and yearned over them without the least hope of possession. And now, they were hers, but the tresses that should have adorned the coveted adornments were gone.

But she hugged them to her bosom, and at length she was able to look up with dim eyes and a smile and say: "My hair grows so fast, Jim!"

And then Della leaped up like a little singed cat and cried, "Oh, oh!"

Jim had not yet seen his beautiful present. She held it out to him eagerly upon her open palm. The dull precious metal seemed to flash with a reflection of her bright and ardent spirit.

"Isn't it a dandy, Jim? I hunted all over town to find it. You'll have to look at the time a hundred times a day now. Give me your watch. I want to see how it looks on it."

Instead of obeying, Jim tumbled down on the couch and put his hands under the back of his head and smiled.

"Dell," said he, "let's put our Christmas presents away

and keep 'em a while. They're too nice to use just at present.
I sold the watch to get the money to buy your combs. And
now suppose you put the chops on."

The magi, as you know, were wise men—wonderfully wise
men—who brought gifts to the Babe in the manger. They
invented the art of giving Christmas presents. Being wise,
their gifts were no doubt wise ones, possibly bearing the
privilege of exchange in case of duplication. And here I
have lamely related to you the uneventful chronicle of two
foolish children in a flat who most unwisely sacrificed for
each other the greatest treasures of their house. But in a
last word to the wise of these days let it be said that of all
who give gifts these two were the wisest. Of all who give
and receive gifts, such as they are wisest. Everywhere they
are wisest. They are the magi.

CPSIA information can be obtained
at www.ICGtesting.com
Printed in the USA
BVHW060237150620
581364BV00003B/14